Broken Cities
Katy Evans-Bush

smith|doorstop

Published 2017 by
smith|doorstop books
The Poetry Business
Bank Street Arts
32–40 Bank Street
Sheffield S1 2DS

Copyright © Katy Evans-Bush 2017
All Rights Reserved

ISBN 978-1-910367-79-7
Typeset by Utter
Printed by People for Print, Sheffield

smith|doorstop books are a member of Inpress:
www.inpressbooks.co.uk. Distributed by NBN International, Airport Business Centre, 10 Thornbury Road Plymouth PL6 7PP

The Poetry Business gratefully acknowledges the support of Arts Council England.

Contents

5	Don't Look Down
6	The Milk God
8	Wise Guys Lounge
10	The Broken City
11	To the Sea Party
12	The Great Illness
13	Snowing
14	Croonerisms
18	The Republican Convention 2008
19	Poem in Which Fashion is a Vacuum
20	East London Song; or, Take Me to Your Hipsters
23	Salvation Stations
24	Field of Fire, 1555
26	The Martyr's Catechism
28	Prior Bolton's Oriel Window
30	A Dark Day in Smithfields
31	The People
32	Plenitude
34	Acknowledgements

For Morgan, Cambria and Danny

Don't Look Down

Oh and then it stops. The cars seize up mid-track.
Don't look down. Don't look back
at the people you were a minute ago, where time and movement merge
on some crazy axis, where the verge
of up meets the cusp of down and blue is red
and violet rose and sugar and the engine's dead
and kisses are sweet and love is said
to be the Word

and anyway all their faces are blurred.
And the track is gone in front and the side disappears below
and the you behind you's laughing, what does *you* know,
and the countryside's a hole. Yes, a hole. Black,
sucking matter into anti-matter, in that nothing matters, and some whack
job has painted over all the trees again
and okay it will wash off in the rain but there isn't any rain,
or wait. There is nothing but rain,

and the fairground people slip in the mud, and the nothing
that is something is no different from the nothing that is not
and you are mysteriously alone in your roller coaster car,
alone behind the locked locked locked locked bar,
and now there is probably a clown.
I said: don't look down.

The Milk God

At first the milk doesn't even know it's happening.
It didn't get put back in the fridge one day.
It spends a night on the counter.
Maybe it was already a little off, who knows.

By the time it's grown a layer of clear whey
there's another bottle sitting nearby,
beginning to feel warm in its exposed position.
Milk bottles are useful for watering plants, you know.

By the time the second one's layer of whey
is glowing a little in the light from the window,
the first has curds inside, and the dog's abandoned
dish on the floor below is really smelling.

Next to the sink sits the granddaddy, the sun,
of all milk bottles. This mighty being
stands tall and kind of bearded, his translucent plastic
body almost mystical. Visible inside him

where it radiates heat, and the smell that forms their atmosphere,
is the source of his power: a hardened orb
of golden orange. Beneath it, a primordial swamp
of the raw elixir of life has shrivelled and congealed.

Around him in all directions, his acolytes
are a growing band. Slender and clear, with contents
white, cream, yellow, they accede to the natural order,
to the great one in whose ways they can't but follow.

Their universe expands, the gospel of their stench
has claimed the kitchen and the living room, and the doorway
to the garden, which is a tangle of weeds, dead staked-up tomatoes,
cat sick, scattered milk bottles, and old cans.

Anne at Social Services – an agnostic, or a creationist –
respects neither evolution nor transubstantiation,
nor the power and glory of the heat of the golden ball.
She says, 'One old man had 250.' And ends the call.

Wise Guys Lounge

Here dust, receipts, bags, circulars, old cheese,
dog snacks, settle into a sedimentary
post-apocalyptic stillness.
No year, no postcode, no expiry date
means anything in this place where time has warped.
But touch with your finger a plastic wrapper,
an old congealed bean tin, a forgotten bag,
a box inside a box or full of boxes,
and a million tiny *somethings* will come out –
grubbing for their share of life.

Upstairs the people untwist a hanger,
worry it down the wall through bricks and plaster
and use it to hold your curtain open
so their friends can look in and laugh.
Sometimes strange hands just reach straight through
and hold the curtain open. It's by your bed.
There's no chink, but other nights you see
through the curtain itself the teeth that glint
in open mouths, acid in the street light.
Lately they've had parties in the garden.
No one talks to you but they say your name;
They try to steal the dog. They change the cat,
who grows first white, then thin, then dies.

Little black specks fly in from the garden.
Electronic zappers from catalogues do nothing,
the flies avoid them.
Instead they lounge around the fridge
like wise guys, and fall in when you open the door;
they come to rest in planetary seas
that form round volcanic islands of rotting meat,
and slowly sink below the oceanic pink.
Some fall down instead
into the freezer, where they freeze.

The Broken City

Their bony silver weight on your lap,
their unlovely yowling,
their eyes and their despot hearts opaque:
Kitty, Kitty, Kitty, Kitti, 'Kittitu' –
the spellings more bizarre in recent years –
and the dove-striped tom and his brother,
sons of Mehitabel. Mehitabel herself, the childlike
stray who died of cat flu in the next-door garden
a week after giving birth to a litter of kittens.
Where lie their bones?
                              Why, out beside the shed,
behind the raised bed. Some in brass-plaqued urns.
And Charley – beautiful and heroic Spitz,
as plush and rosy as the cats were not,
has vanished barking into your private ether.
                                          You sit aloft
on your electric barque as on a dais –
raised on high by means of a remote –
and drink weak tea from the spout of a plastic cup,
your wall adorned with flower-calendar pages.
You can't perceive them, ghostly presences.
Trapped in the broken city in your desert
of buckled synapses and zapped neurons,
the drought and then the sandstorm that collapsed them,
the cats slide unperceived, imperious,
and there poor Charley wags and barks, forgotten.

Other ghostly presences, however,
you do perceive.
                      Who are those people? you ask,
pointing a finger at the foot of your bed.

To the Sea Party

Go that far down and you're moving through night:
you part the world's lead-liquid atmosphere –
last particles of oxygen collapse –
and see nothing. You're blacked out past your red,
your bluey-grey, your scales or skin or frond.
Passing squid provide your only outerwear,
from who can see where.

Further down, the smaller crustaceans are their day.
Phosphorescence flashes while they dance
like Gatsby in colour and never stop. The noctiluca
form in tiny shining swarms and are both canapé
and Chinese lantern. It's their party. Down here
you eat the prey that shines, while you shine on your prey.

The Great Illness
i.m. MCB

The world holds him in its softening
afternoon light, his elbows
stuck at angles, his hands like clay
hands on cold arms. He is out of keeping
with everything. Everywhere
everyday objects scrape and push and clatter;
their effort escapes him. So even the tiny leaves
can flutter on their tiny green stems
along confusing golden acacia branches,
what do they know?
                              Statesman of nothing,
he inhabits alone his magnificent
wheelchair, his steel carriage with its tall black collar.
He rests his head back. He sits. There is a clot in his heart,
on its splendid red throne among the gold-tipped dignitaries.

Snowing
i.m. MCB

The next afternoon, and snow is falling.
Unreal weather. What was black and grey
the previous day has turned to grey and white.

Already Dad's dust must be sinking down,
politely sociable among habitual elements,
working the particled soil like a room.

Each ash-flake seeks accommodation
among the noisy minerals, until
it finds that private no-place underneath

the unlit memorial garden, until it finds
the muffled reception, the under-party, the ultimate
winter mixer, where there is always snow falling.

Croonerisms

Dean Martin
was no Spartan.
Eyes like a pizza pies, he was so starry
when he sang 'Volaré'.

❊

Perry Como
sang in slo-mo.
He slo-mo'ed the ladies from Honolulu to Toledo
in his tuxedo.

❊

Bing
sure could sing:
it made him so rich he could afford to spend all his Christmases
on isthmuses.

❊

Desi Arnaz
sez
his family's unimaginable luxury was stolen by the Cuban revolutionaries,
so he goes to America and joins the crooning luminaries.

Lucille Ball,
on the other hand, has it all:
she's the beautiful loon the crooner marries.

❊

Now, the thing about unimaginable luxury
is that we imagine it all the time, we
manufacture it, we inhabit it, we make it
tame: our hi-fi record players croon for us
from the corners of air conditioned rooms
over spindle-legged tables spread for bridge, over which
martini glasses travel hand to mouth and dust-dry olives
enter the mouths of men in Dino Martin glasses,
men who talk of crowns and bridgework while their wives,
their coiffed and romantic wives,
plan what to do with the kids by the pool tomorrow.

❂

Waiter, waiter, escalator,
salad lunch and golfing later.

Voice like Marsala, lyrics like honey;
there's no zero-sum game like money.

And may all your Christmases be white,
and may all your isthmuses be white-capped.

Luxury never lasts. Real life bursts in,
the pool springs a leak and everything must be paid for. Fade to poor.

❂

Even the pool-sweeper dreams of swimming with the card sharks,
sitting on replica Louis Quatorze with a woman he can only imagine
in black and white, or showered with light;
he imagines drinking something pink with bubbles, while some crooner
sits singing on the stage. It's the very stage we're merely players on,
but the sweeper is out of luck. He imagines things

while he sweeps, while he sleeps. No running by the poolside.
What a shmuck.

❂

Sinatra and Davis Jr –
croony and croonier –
did it their way with expensive predilections
and good connections.

The whole rat pack
patted the racks
of many a passing dame.
That was their game.

❂

Oh, crooning is a form of nostalgia.
The idea of luxury is a form of nostalgia.
Summertime is a form of nostalgia,
the 6am swim, the pool a giant dewdrop in a drenched and silent garden,
the barbecue among privately owned trees,
the windows with gold silk drapes drawn in against the sun,
the sun itself in which the skin and the heart both harden.
Suntans are a form of nostalgia.
Optimism is a form of nostalgia.
Nostalgia is a form of nostalgia.
Turn me loose, what's the use?
Money is a form of neuralgia.

❂

Tony Soprano
plays the piano.
He's a different kind of crooner, it seems:
he croons for screams.

Tony Soprano
at the piano
plays like there's no tomorrow.
There is no tomorrow.

The Republican Convention 2008

'All those people and the way
they talked I hope they don't all
take their guns when they go to see Obama –
I wouldn't be surprised if they do

! You should have heard them all
cheering 'Obama doesn't deserve
to be president' I think they said but the main
thing was they had flies all over their faces – thousands
of tiny specks, they were everywhere so it was
no surprise when two little hands
reached from behind someone's head with all
their fingers waving right there
in the TV trying to kill the flies

it was most disturbing I can tell you
the flies and the cheering and the guns'

Poem in Which Fashion is a Vacuum

Vanta Black, fifties chanteuse,
was a killer in her little black dress.
Most girls wore feathers, or silk of chartreuse,
but she simply sucked out the light to impress.

East London Song; or, Take Me to Your Hipsters
after Kurt Weill

Well, show me the way
To the next hipster bar.
  Oh, don't ask why.
  Oh, don't ask why.

Show me the way
To the most whiskered bard.
  Oh, he won't shave;
  Oh don't ask why.

For if we don't find
The next hipster bar,
In bitcoins we can't pay;
In Shoreditch we will die.
  I tell you, I text you,
  I tell you we must die.

Sing me Kurt Vile
In the next hipster bar.
  Oh, don't ask why.
  Oh, you know why.

Oh, moon of dear old Hoxton,
We now must say goodbye:
  We've lost our sense of purpose
  And need hipsters to show us why.

Oh, moon of Dalston Junction,
It's good morning, not goodbye.
  We've missed our good old night bus,
  We need espresso, oh, you know why.

Show me the link
To the best hipster URL,
  It will lead the way.
  It will lead the way.

Oh, retro moon of London,
How analogue you are!
  We lost all our signal,
  Down in the cellar bar.

Oh, moon of old Stoke Newington,
We ne'er must say goodbye.
  You shine on our old-style Instagrams;
  We need filters, don't ask why.

The moon shines over Clapton
And we now must say goodbye.
  Some of us live in Walthamstow
  (though some would rather die).

Well, show me the way
To the next lo-fi bar.
  The wood's all ply,
  The wood's all ply.

For if we don't find
A plaid-shirted earl
I tell you we must lie,
And tell them it's this guy.
  They'll trust you. I'll text you.
  I tell you, we must lie.

Show me the place
Where the real hipsters are.
  They don't ask why,
  They don't care why.

Oh, moon of Lea Bridge Roundabout
Like bunting in the sky:
  We've lost our good old Rastas,
  And must have hipsters, oh, who knows why.

Salvation Stations

Dear Jesus,
I am fucking exhausted.
I'm writing you this note
from the second circle of hell
which is the Bakerloo Line
on a dark Thursday evening in January.
The next station will be the City of Dis.

The first of my circles
was that meeting with the lawyer.
He says I shouldn't have done it
but he understands and he's not
going to kick up a fuss. Salvation takes
many forms here in the underworld.
I am, sincerely, yours, at a different station.

Field of Fire, 1555

In this city
three digits the same means fire.

John Leaf (aged twenty years), apprentice
to Mr Humphrey Gaudy, tallow-chandler,
suffered and was himself turned to tallow
at Smithfield on 12th July with Rev John Bradford.

Brought to this place and led down these grey flags
while the air shimmered its summer welcome.
Into the public place, to a weeping
multitude gathered overnight to stand with them.

And John Leaf and the good Rev Bradford suffered
out here by this traffic bollard –
as it was said, which was a great comfort, *like two lambs,
without any alteration of their countenance.*

Said the Reverend Bradford, *Be of good comfort, brother,
for we shall have a merry supper with the Lord this night.*

It was reported, says Dr Fox, that when
they showed him his confession to sign,
he took a pin and signed it with his blood,
to show the bishop he had sealed the deed.

The flames held them like twin cups of – well, like twin
cups of London fire. Out here on the traffic island. Thus
they offered themselves like drinks to the thirsty Lord,
and wound, as lilac smoke does, from His cup.

Tell that to the guy who's refused a final pint
by the barman in the Bishop's Finger at closing time.
A streetlight flickers and dies, and the sky goes black,
and somebody pricks himself on a pin, goes *fuck!*
and wipes it on his jeans or a leaf from the pavement;
and somebody else can't get a cab, and the last tube's gone,
and a slight, sickly smell of kebabs and tar lingers.

The Martyr's Catechism

In extreme times,
extreme dreams.

Braced for eternity,
finds grace.

Grace in extremity.
Extreme as it seems,

to suffer is the act
actively sought

its pagan Latin *ferre* –
to bear –

gladly given to
God's fire.

Extreme reward:
from tract to deed.

Heaven hovers
over all the air,

the faintest coloration:
red, or violet?

The truth is hard.
God shows no face.

Let the fire be
your catechism.

He is content
to be your prism.

Prior Bolton's Oriel Window

Meanwhile, in the priory at Great St Bart's,
Prior Bolton's oriel window, with its central motif –
a barrel, or tun – pierced with a bolt.
(Take a moment for the wit to sink in.)
Through these beautiful panes, among cushions,
the aging prior, and Clerk of Works to the King,
kept an eye on mass, and on his monks
at prayer and reflection in the cloisters.

His servants looked to the books, and he to King Henry,
to God, to contractors, and to other matters,
and kept things running with virtue and no fuss.
A wise and canny man.
                            The question is raised
whether wiser *when he invented for his name*
a bird-bolt through his Tun, writes William Camden,
or when he built him a house upon Harrow Hill –
well out of the city, when the panic of '26
drove the wealthy to flee the waters of Heaven –
for fear of an inundation after a great
conjunction of planets in the watery triplicity.
Imagine it, Bolton safe on dry land,
while below him the monks, fools, sinners are all drowned.

It never comes to pass, of course, but the Prior
was entirely in the right: had the floods
indeed risen to devour the city,
his monks in their pure and spiritually cleansed state
would have ascended joyfully at the hands of angels
from Great St Bart's straight to Heaven.
                                      Have a think

of King Henry's practical Prior when you sit and watch
the daily trumpetings of internet or telly.
Through this glass we see our own Prior Boltons,
and they see us, with their data-gathering technology.

A Dark Day in Smithfields

On this Smooth Field
Wat Tyler died,

stabbed with a sword
by the Mayor of London

while the boy Edward
sat on his horse, and witnessed.

Across Europe all the kings
watched, for their own business.

The peasants are revolting, sire.
To cover up the memory of Wat,

paved over, built over,
and washed in the stenches of death,

Smithfield has ever since worked for its living.
Said the Wizard of Id: *I'll say they are!*

The People

But what is either a phantom, or a person, but a spirit
that's taken on corporeal form?
By these ghostly things, then, by this fine checked
sleeve, tiny stitched buttons fabric-covered & delicate
by its shape holding although long ripped
& by this mitten somebody's mother knitted
& by this wimpled face of a girl grinning down through an open window,
& by this hairbrush, & by this hairpin,
& by a child's tiny knight-on-a-horse
& by a wooden cock a hoop
& by a top atop a wooden top
& by the kitten Gyb, you can see
we are alive, you know, we are living.

Please scratch here
Pls scrtch

Plenitude
after Gabriel Moreno

It's crazy to know that things are possible.
You do not even need to believe one hundred per cent
in potentiality
to go around making the nights
a little more bearable and beautiful,
because they already are more bearable and beautiful
somewhere, anyway.

And most of the time it's not really our fault
that plenitude does not happen.
It was there all the time. it was bitten off by chance,
by the dogs of fate.
Fuck me!
I would prefer that it had been my fault.

Acknowledgements

Poems in this pamphlet originally appeared in the following: *Ambit, The London Column, PN Review, Poems in Which,* and *Poetry Wales.*

'Croonerisms' was written for and first performed at a reading in Farringdon run by Roddy Lumsden in the summer of 2015.

'Poem in Which Fashion is a Vacuum' has also appeared in the anthology *Findings on Light*, published by the Pars Foundation, 2016.

'Don't Look Down' was featured in 'Call of the Wild', an exhibition at Studio Ex Purgamento, London, in 2016.

None of us is an island. We rely on the moral support, practical help, critical expertise, generosity and time of our colleagues and friends. My thanks go to Astrid Alben, David Secombe, Natalia Zagorska-Thomas, Gabriel Moreno, John Clegg and AB Jackson, among others.

Big thanks are also due to the Society of Authors and the Royal Literary Fund for helping to make this possible.